Y0-CAH-406

Puppy School

by Diana Noonan
illustrated by Lee Krutop

Harcourt
SCHOOL PUBLISHERS

Printed in Mexico

ISBN 10: 0-15-349975-3
ISBN 13: 978-0-15-349975-3

Ordering Options
ISBN 10: 0-15-349937-0 (Grade 2 ELL Collection)
ISBN 13: 978-0-15-349937-1 (Grade 2 ELL Collection)
ISBN 10: 0-15-357212-4 (package of 5)
ISBN 13: 978-0-15-357212-8 (package of 5)

2 3 4 5 6 7 8 9 10   050   15 14 13 12 11 10 09 08 07

Jemma is taking her puppy to
puppy school.

Puppies and their owners learn to work together at puppy school.

Jemma calls her puppy Sam.
Sam loves to play with a ball,
but he can't play today.

Today Jemma will teach Sam
some tricks.

"Are you ready, Sam?"
asks Jemma.

Sam listens to Jemma.

"Sit," says Jemma.

She gently pushes Sam down
onto his back legs.

"Stay," says Jemma.

Sam stays where he is.

Sam learns to stay when Jemma
walks away from him.

Sam also learns to walk beside Jemma.

Sam learns to lie down, too.

Sam can do the tricks!
He is a good puppy.

Scaffolded Language Development

CONCEPT WORDS Write each of the following words on a card: *puppy, tricks, teach, sit, stay.* Ask children to read each word and discuss its meaning. Then write the sentence frames below on the board. (Make sure each word space on the board is large enough for children to insert the correct word card.) Read each sentence and help children choose the card with the concept word that correctly completes the sentence. Then have a child place the word card in the space, and have children chorally read the completed sentence.

1. It takes time to learn ___.
2. I teach my puppy to __ and ___.
3. My new ___ is very cute.
4. It is fun to ___ my puppy.

🍁 Science

Draw and Label Discuss with children the life cycle of a dog. Then guide children in drawing each stage of the life cycle. Have them write labels for each stage.

School-Home Connection

Dog Training Ask children to talk about the book with family members. Then talk about why it is important that pet dogs are trained.

Word Count: 108